The Trojan Women

A DRAMA ADAPTED BY

Ellen McLaughlin

FROM THE PLAY BY EURIPIDES

The Rules in Brief

- DO NOT perform this Play without obtaining prior permission from Playscripts, and without paying the required royalty.

- DO NOT photocopy, scan, or otherwise duplicate any part of this book.

- DO NOT alter the text of the Play, change a character's gender, delete any dialogue, cut any music, or alter any objectionable language, unless explicitly authorized by Playscripts.

- DO provide the required credit to the author(s) and the required attribution to Playscripts in all programs and promotional literature associated with any performance of this Play.

Copyright Basics

This Play is protected by United States and international copyright law. These laws ensure that authors are rewarded for creating new and vital dramatic work, and protect them against theft and abuse of their work.

A play is a piece of property, fully owned by the author, just like a house or car. You must obtain permission to use this property, and must pay a royalty fee for the privilege—whether or not you charge an admission fee. Playscripts collects these required payments on behalf of the author.

Anyone who violates an author's copyright is liable as a copyright infringer under United States and international law. Playscripts and the author are entitled to institute legal action for any such infringement, which can subject the infringer to actual damages, statutory damages, and attorneys' fees. A court may impose statutory damages of up to $150,000 for willful copyright infringements. U.S. copyright law also provides for possible criminal sanctions. Visit the website of the U.S. Copyright Office (www.copyright.gov) for more information.

THE BOTTOM LINE: If you break copyright law, you are robbing a playwright and opening yourself to expensive legal action. Follow the rules, and when in doubt, ask us.

Cast of Characters

CHORUS, a minimum of six women ranging in age from teenagers to elderly, the remnants of the citizens of Troy, including Hecuba's retinue.

POSEIDON, a god, middle aged.

HECUBA, a queen, middle aged.

HELEN, a beauty, ageless.

CASSANDRA, a prophet, 20s.

ANDROMACHE, a mother, 20s-30s.

TALTHYBIUS, a Greek soldier, 20s-30s.

Setting

The shoreline below the conquered city of Troy.

Author's Notes

The Trojan Women was written in response to the Bosnian War in 1995 and originally was cast with people from the former Yugoslavia and Albania living in New York, many of them refugees from the war. Even with a cast who had no acting training and whose English skills were minimal, we found that the ancient power of Euripides' text spoke clearly of the timeless sorrow and suffering of the victims of war. In that production each part was performed by more than one actor and those actors were often people from different sides of the conflict collaborating by necessity to perform a character together. The actors spoke some of the text in English and some in their own language, using their own translations, overlapping and dovetailing their words with the other actors playing the part. I welcome this kind of approach and designed the text to be lean enough to support that. But I've also seen more conventional productions and believe it works equally effectively either way. The key is simplicity and clarity. I've found that attempts to update the piece in any obvious way tend to reduce it rather than illuminate it and that design elements are most effective when they are minimal and evocative rather than literal and specific.

Acknowledgments

The Trojan Women was developed through the Balkan Theater Project with support from the Lila-Wallace—Reader's Digest Fund. It was presented in a staged reading at New York City's Classic Stage Company (David Esbjornson, Artistic Director; Patricia Taylor, managing Director) in association with American Friends Service Committee on June 17, 1996. The director was Ellen McLaughlin, the co-director was Ivan Talijancic; Sarilee Kahn was collaborator, Jack Patterson was the administrator and Amy Stern was the stage manager. The cast was as follows:

POSEIDON . . . . Ensar Halilovic, Marko Maglich
HECUBA . . . . Justina Aliaj, Azra Fazlic-Dujmovic,
Nada Selimovic
CASSANDRA . . . . Taida Horozovic, Azra Sisic,
Selma Subasic
ANDROMACHE . . . . Svetlana Ardi, Elma Balic
TALTHYBIUS . . . . Luan Begetti, Igor Hadzismajlovic
THE CHORUS . . . . Maja Brajic, Fatima Djekic,
Sandra Hadzismajlovic, Sandra Miocic,
Jasmina Omerovic, Edina Sarajlic
Elza Zagreda, Lejla Zvisdic

THE TROJAN WOMEN
adapted by Ellen McLaughlin

FROM THE PLAY BY EURIPIDES

(The stage is empty except for a group of women asleep on the ground. They are the last of the WOMEN OF TROY, *some of them in the remnants of what were once ornate garments since they made up the retinue of the queen. Some are in more modest clothing. All are refugees. In the center is the queen,* HECUBA. POSEIDON *enters. He looks at the sleeping women.)*

POSEIDON.
I am Poseidon. Stepped up from my element, the sea, to walk
one last time on the broken streets of the only city I ever loved.
Troy. What have they done to you?
Your gentle gates. Your tall trees. Your fine spires.
All gone. A ruin. A memory of a great city.   5
Another war has ended. When will the next begin?

(In all the chorus sections, the WOMEN *split the lines among them. The* WOMEN *speak in their sleep. Care should be taken, particularly in these early sleep-talking sections, that the choral voice be seamless and musical, the speakers occasionally dovetailing and overlapping each other so that the voices meld.)*

WOMEN.
I dream of a city.
My home.
I am a mother there.
I am a sister   10
I am a wife.
I am a daughter.
I am a fine craftswoman.
I heal the sick.
I carry milk from my goats on the hills.   15
I know everyone.
I sell herbs.
I am an artist.
I paint fine drawings on slender vases.
I am a great beauty.   20
I am a gossip.
So many stories to tell.

POSEIDON.
And all these women, these sleeping mothers, wives and daughters,
Become trophies, spoils, baggage.

WOMEN.
The smoke curls from morning fires.   25
The song of the fishmongers in the early light.
The scent of flowers on the ledge.
The streets.
The streets.
The streets.   30
Curving up the hills from the sea.
Echoing voices.
Laughter.
Talk.
Children's games.   35
Tradesmen's yells.
Dogs barking.
Cooking smells circling from all the hearth fires.
All the families.
All the children fed.   40
Such a city.
Such a city.
Such a city.
My home.
My home.   45
My home.
Every corner.
Every stone of every street.
I know it like the back of my hand.
Like the roof of my mouth.   50
Like the colors I find on the back of my closed eyelids.
It was mine.
It was mine.
It was mine.
I dream of a city.   55
My home.

POSEIDON. *(Locating* HECUBA*:)*
Even she, who was the queen.
Nothing now. A lot cast in the game of endings.
Odysseus, they say, drew her.
He who devised the Trojan Horse,   60
that cunning and terrible trick.
He will drag the queen of Troy home in a saddle bag
to toss before his patient wife.

Don't wake up, Lady.
Whatever you dream, even the most horrifying dream   65
Cannot be worse than what you will awake to.
Here is the end of meaning.
Here is loss beyond comprehension.

HECUBA. *(Asleep:)*
In a moment a stone will be thrown at the sleeping
crows. They will flap upwards, shocked from their home on   70
the ground. They will circle upon each other, screaming,
twisting the air like rope. At the center of this coil of wings,
I am the blackest crow, the mother of all the confused and lost.
It will be for me to make order from this chaos. Our flight will
be eternal, for sustenance we will eat the wind.   75
Stay the hand that throws the stone. One more moment. Just
one more moment let us weigh the soft, ordinary dirt with our
accustomed bodies.

POSEIDON.
Oh, sleep.
Sleep a little longer.   80
From the moment you wake until your deaths
You will be exiles.

> (POSEIDON *exits.* HELEN *appears. She walks among the
> sleeping bodies. She is exquisitely dressed, in vivid contrast
> to the women she steps around. Her long hair is beautifully
> coiffed.)*

HELEN.
I too loved Troy.
Like you, soon I will stand at the back of a ship and watch
the smoking shore disappear from view, remembering the   85
beauty of the city I brought to ruin. The sound of her
        fountains,
the songbirds that graced her rustling, fragrant gardens, the
fruits that bobbed in the gentle breeze of her orchards. All this
I will think of as the sails belly us away and we drag a snake of
foam behind our sharp prows. Soon what's left of her will be   90
lost to the gray waves. All that will remain is the memory.
Such a city.
The city I came to destroy.

> (HELEN *exits.* HECUBA *wakes.)*

HECUBA.
My Troy!
Cross roads and shade trees!   95

Market places and schools!
Graves of my ancestors!
Wake, my women!
Today is our death!
Lift up your heads!   100
Rise and be slaves.

(The WOMEN *wake, disoriented.*)

WOMEN.
My queen, why do you wake us?
What's the matter?
Where are we?
Why are we here?   105
Is the queen upset?
Oh, the dream I had!
I remember they brought us here last night.
I'm shivering.
Is it cold or is it fright?   110
Where is my brother?... Oh, of course.
I remember now.
I remember now.
I remember now.
The war.   115
The war.
Our ruined city.
Our scattered families.
All the wounded.
All the maddened ones.   120
All the dead.
I thought I might have dreamed it.
Oh, the dream I had.
I thought it might have been a dream.
I keep thinking I'll wake up from it.   125
And then we wake to this.

HECUBA.
Day is breaking and with it, our lives.
Today the fleet will leave and we will go with it to Greece.
Today we leave our home and each other
We scatter, each alone, to our fates   130
We will be strangers in a foreign land forever after.

WOMEN.
I can't even imagine it.
Places I've only heard of.
Argos...The Islands...Sparta

I once went to Greece. It was a long time ago. A great house   135
at the foot of Olympus, the holy mountain. It was really quite
beautiful. No one was poor or hungry. It was so warm.
The ground smelled good. Like bread.

It might not be so bad.
What do you mean? We will be slaves!   140
Prostitutes.
Spat on.
I don't know the languages, they'll laugh at me.
They'll kick you first.
No bruises, we are prizes.   145
Beauties.
Whores.
I will be homesick for the rest of my life.
I'm already homesick, my home doesn't exist anymore.

Perhaps we shall sail past Greece and west to Africa.   150
They say it never rains there and the earth has turned to sand.
And I've heard of Sicily.
The mountains are cool
It's covered with forests
And in the plains the grass grows up to your waist.   155
I think they would welcome us in Sicily.
They say if you wash your hair in their rivers it
          comes out gold.
Gold dust.
What are you talking about?
Don't be a fool.   160
Gold, they said.

What is that fire?
Look, a blaze!
What terrible brightness comes here?
Is the city on fire?   165

HECUBA. No, it is just a girl, but her mind is aflame.

CASSANDRA. *(Offstage:)*
Burn high! Burn strong!
Burn bright! Burn long!

HECUBA.
Oh, look on her, and let her break your heart.
It is my mad daughter.   170
My beautiful Cassandra.

          (CASSANDRA *enters, dressed in white, garlanded, carry-*
          ing a torch.)

CASSANDRA.
Enter the bride! Happy, happy day!
Where are the dancers? Where are the singers?
Where are my maiden friends to swell the procession?
Dance me now, sing me now, to my bright burning bed.   175
I, lucky child, to be the Queen of Greece!
Lucky virgin, to trade my priestess veil
for the wedding garland.
King Agamemnon calls for me!
The king himself!   180
Blood of my brothers washed from his hands
He calls the queen's mad daughter to his groaning bed.
In his bloated ship, laden with my city's jewels,
pans and brooches
He calls to take me, mad me, across the sea   185
to his neglected kingdom and his murderous wife.
That wife, that mother of his child
whose throat he slit
to appease the Goddess
to blow the winds   190
to set the sails
to bring the army to our walls
to sack the city
to kill my family
all those ten years ago.   195
That wife.
Home to her! With mad me in the crook of his arm!
Happy, happy day!
Raise the torch high!

HECUBA.
Oh, my poor child. You don't know what you're saying. You are   200
still in the power of Apollo who loved you and cursed you at once.

CASSANDRA.
Happy day!
Happy Trojans!

HECUBA. You can't mean what you're saying.

CASSANDRA.
Ah, but I do. Poor blind Greeks.   205
Their general, so wise, killed his favorite daughter to come here,
to waste his best years, watching his men die on our beaches,
far from home. Their children that were babies when they left
grew up without them, learned how to walk, how to speak, run,
play, write and read (ten years is a long time) all without them.   210

And while the fathers threw themselves against the walls
of our city, as those years passed, sons and daughters forgot
their father's face, forgot their father's touch, his smell, the
sound of his voice, until they found they seldom thought
of him—almost never, in fact—and always without much feeling.   215
And they watch their mothers grow old and uncertain.
Not knowing if they are widows or not, the years go by.
The poor Greeks! Our conquerors! Homesick and tired,
eternally squabbling, mending their armor, stealing from each
other, squinting out from our beaches across the water   220
over which they came so long ago and for what?
Some wandered wife? Some faded adulteress?
For whom they lay down their lives for ten long years, sand in
their beds, meal after wretched army meal, days and months
and season after season. These are the men you fear?   225
Pity them!

And pity most of all the bridegroom general.
Agamemnon.
For when he carries me with him, he carries his death.
The ax is on him. And on mad me.   230
Oh, yes, I am there, naked beside him in the open grave.
I see us both.
But we shall both be dead.

(She kneels, knocks on the earth and listens.)

Are you there, my father? Are you there, my brothers?
I'm coming. I'm coming.   235
Where is the bridegroom? My stamping general?
Here is the bride! Here is the bride!

(CASSANDRA exits.)

HECUBA.
Oh, Apollo! She was your favorite. Is this your ecstasy? Is this
your blessing? Raving and laughing as she goes to her death?
What can it mean to be a favorite of such a god?   240
Have all the gods gone mad? What kind of world is this?
Women, help me. Sing.

WOMEN.
What shall we sing about?
Sing of the horse.
Yes, sing of the horse.   245
The way we saw it,
so high and silent,
out on the beach in the early morning.

Dawn streaking its mighty flanks pink
How tall it was!   250
Higher than the walls of the city.
And its enormous glittering eyes.
The smile carved on its lips.
Its long black legs
Its ribs hooped like the hull of a ship   255
Its curving neck
Its massive head
Oh, we wanted it inside with us.
And as they dragged it in we sang
All the songs we hadn't sung since before the war   260
We danced around it in the square
Peace, we thought
With this beautiful wooden gift at the center
Bonfires burning all night long
All over the city   265
And instruments played that we'd almost forgotten how to play
It had been so long
The children were up so late
But how could you keep them in bed?
Everyone was so happy   270
At last.

        And when sleep finally came
        You slept to the fading sounds of a rejoicing city
        I thought: This is the first night we shall all sleep together
        in peacetime. My husband beside me. I thought: 275
                praise God,
        he is still alive. We have survived the war intact. All of us.
        Praise God. And I slept. Curled beside him. Smiling.
        I woke when the children came to the bed. Their hands
                were cold.
        They were trembling. "The Greeks", they said,
        "The Greeks have come out of the horse!"   280
Who could believe it?
Who could believe it?
And the black wave of death swallowed the city
Coursed in rivers down the streets
Through open windows   285
Overturned all the cradles
Tipped all the spires
Cracked the walls
And we lost everything
Just when we thought we'd saved it forever.   290

Nothing more cruel
Nothing more terrible
Than hope
Hope
Followed by such darkness   295
A night we still wander in
Calling the names of our husbands
Our lovers
Our friends
Our children   300

> (HELEN *enters. Silence. The* WOMEN *move from her with
> contempt.*)

HECUBA.
Was it only yesterday you were still my subject? Only
yesterday when you still had to watch me from your place
at the long table and wait until I raised my glass before
you could begin to drink? How long ago it seems.
And how like you, coward that you are, to wait until we   305
are reduced to chattel, slaves at auction,
before you dare to walk among us.

HELEN.
Slavery is new to you. No wonder you chafe at it. When you've
endured it as long as I have, years and years, you'll learn to
stand up to it without so much self-pity.   310
And then you'll know what I have had to bear.

HECUBA. What have you ever borne besides a lover's weight?

HELEN.
The contempt of the world.
You'll know soon enough. When you rise from your raping
beds, wiping your eyes and smoothing your skirts down over   315
your thighs now purple with your new master's handprints,
perhaps you'll think of me. When you run from your
conquerors and find no mercy anywhere, only veiled eyes,
turned heads and snickering; when servants, children and
strangers on the street spit at you and call you a whore,   320
then, then, oh, I hope you think of me.

HECUBA.
You actually expect sympathy from us? You, who never drew
a breath that didn't cause an innocent person pain?

HELEN.
I gave up on sympathy long ago. How can anyone understand
what it is to live in the remorseless noon light of this endless 325

visibility? Always I've been watched and judged. Run through
by the gazes of gods and men. I've never known the cool shadow
of privacy, never known anything like ordinary kindness.

HECUBA.
And you accuse me of self-pity.
What can your petty vanities mean here? Look at the cost   330
of your little drama and weigh your words.
We may be slaves, but we still have the freedom to take our
justice as we find it. What can keep us from having our
revenge now that you are finally helpless against our hatred
and without protection?   335

HELEN.
When have I ever had protection?
This is so familiar.
And hatred?
It's all I've ever known.
Bought and bundled one bedroom to the next   340
to writhe beneath my many conquerors.

HECUBA. You had your choices.

HELEN.
And you think I would choose this? To be loathed by
the entire world? To be the source of so much misery?
I never had a choice. I was the bride of force.   345
Behind every man who took me stood a goddess
Who steadied his hips and whispered in his ear.

HECUBA.
The shame of your actions can't be blamed on a god.
You saw your chances, you sniffed the air and you went
where the pillows were softest, where the wine was sweetest.   350
What has it cost you? Nothing.

HELEN. I've lost everything.

HECUBA.
What have you lost? What have you ever valued beyond
your own comfort? Your country? You abandoned them to
wretched turmoil only to drag them behind you in your wake   355
to us. Troy? You "love" Troy, perhaps?
Fools that we were, we opened our shining gates to you only
to let you seed your infection of woe in our perfect city.

HELEN. I went where I was taken.

HECUBA.
When the war was feeding at our city's teats and our   360

husbands, sons and brothers were dying, the air shaking with
the keening of women bereft, still you walked the battlements
to flash your hateful beacon of beauty before the sea of troops
and make them writhe and toss into a fury at the sight of you.

HELEN.
I was the cause. My place was there. It was my duty to   365
bear it in public.

HECUBA.
I watched you. Not a flicker of remorse crossed that face
of yours as the massacre raged beneath you. No screams of pain
ever moved you. All our wrack and ruin was reflected in your
unearthly open eyes. Impassive as a bird of prey you looked   370
down upon the awful doings you had brought into the world and
calmly watched the balance of the scales dip and rise with every
death. Which side was winning was all you ever cared to know.

HELEN.
I alone belonged to both sides of the battle. Have you never
thought of that? My face could not betray a preference.   375
There my own blood called, the land of my birth and
childhood, here my adopted country, the most beautiful city
in the world. Every death was a loss, one side or the other,
my heart was in ruins. There was no winning for me.
I was unique in that.   380
I could imagine no victory.

HECUBA.
No victory? Nothing but victory. Either way you won.
Look at you. You came to us unharmed, at the height of your
power and beauty, and now you will be taken home intact.

HELEN.
Of course. I am a piece of property. Something to be stolen,   385
hidden, rescued or restored. A statue. A symbol. Nothing more.

HECUBA.
I cannot even kill you for the pleasure of that justice.
That is for your husband.

HELEN.
You think he'll kill me? After ten years of fighting for me? For
all your wisdom, you know nothing of the truth of men.   390
He will take me back. It is what legend demands. What it has
always demanded. You know that.

HECUBA. I have wasted all my bitterness.

HELEN. It would seem. I did nothing to you.

(Long pause as they stare at each other.)

HECUBA.
If this is the price of beauty, let beauty perish with   395
everything else. Take her and defile her.

(The WOMEN *grab* HELEN *and begin to drag her off.)*

HELEN. *(As she is taken out:)*
What I have was given to me by the gods.
It isn't yours to take from me. It belongs to no one,
least of all to me.
You are fools to hate me. There is no woman here to hate.   400
Only power. And that you cannot skin off of me.
Claw my face to ribbons.
Break these smooth limbs.
Shave my shining hair to stubble.
I will endure.   405

(HELEN is dragged away. HECUBA is alone.)

HECUBA.
What shall become of me? Old bee without a sting. I, who was
the mother of a pride of warriors. Who walked my palace floors
on golden sandals amidst the bobbing of plumed fans.
Shall I watch at a master's door, or sit the night watch for
his coughing child? Might I hold a plate of figs for an   410
idle Greek, standing like a statue as the night wears on,
listening to the drunken talk spiral into babble as the wine
takes hold? Wind a prating girl's ringlet around my bony finger
to curl her hair? Crawl at my mistress' feet to hem her gown?
Shall I turn a spinning wheel or scramble down the dark   415
slope before dawn to carry water from the well? Shall I walk
the dung pile of a back yard, tossing cracked corn to
skittering chickens or sling soapy water across another's floor?
What won't be asked of me? Curled with the dogs on dirty
straw in my corner of the yard, I will hug my rags around me   420
at night and think of the life I had, the city I lost. And perhaps
some day, if I am lucky, I will be past weeping for it. And the
faces of my dead will mottle and blur until they become
indistinct, like stones seen at the bottom of a rushing river bed.

(HELEN is brought back in. Her hair has been hacked off.
She wears a grimy sackcloth dress. Her arms have been
strung on a pole like a scarecrow, her face has been bloodied
with scratches.)

HELEN. *(Laughing:)*
So you think you're free of me now? As if what I am was ever   425

just some body you could shame. You still think I am just some
woman of flesh and bone with a single story? Whoever I might
have been was blasted to nothing long ago in the transforming
furnace of the gods' gaze. That girl was just stick and dung,
fuel to the consuming fire of my fate. The girl you could have   430
punished died long ago.
I became the Helen. The eating flame of beauty.
She happened to the world.
It had nothing to do with me.

HECUBA.
Take her to her husband. Let him see her for what she is.   435
We are done with her. Let him take her. And kill her.
We shall not taint our sacred soil with her blood.

HELEN.
Whatever you dream, you will always be dreaming of her.
Night after night, your city will fall for her. She is the
fire that hollowed you out. She leaves ash and silence and   440
moves on, having blinded.
In your sightless eyes she lingers.
Even as you breathe your last breath
The scent of her will fill your senses.
The shining beauty of her will flood you again.   445
Try to forget me.
You will fail.

(Some of the WOMEN *take her away.)*

HECUBA.
Give her back to her husband. His plucked chicken.
His stranger. Let him take his beauty home.
Andromache!   450

*(*ANDROMACHE *enters with her infant son.)*

ANDROMACHE. Mother! My Queen!

HECUBA.
My brave son's wife! Where are you going?
What do you take with you?

ANDROMACHE.
I go to the Greeks. I take all I have. My son.
Was I a good wife?   455

HECUBA.
He loved you deeply. He called you his shield. There never
was a better wife.

ANDROMACHE.
And that is to be the nature of my punishment. I am given to
the son of my husband's murderer. Achilles' own son claims me.
As his wife. I am to go to his bed. To let him put his arms   460
around me. I am to find comfort there. In the arms, against
the skin of his killer's son. I, who loved a prince.
And they say it is because I was so prized. There was talk.
"A gentle woman," "she who was most intimate with the most
powerful," "she who shared the bed of the greatest hero,"   465
"saw him unmanned in sleep and guarded his naked body with
her own," "she will be the greatest prize."
I see the rest of my life, lived with this stranger,
contracted in sorrow and woe.
How can this be?   470
I am young! I have loved deeply! Shall I never be allowed
to feel anything other than hatred? Isn't that some sort
of crime? To waste a life in hatred? And yet, if I feel
anything else, even an echo of the love and happiness I have
known, I will be betraying my family, my honor, my city,   475
my country.
Perhaps one can only hate a man so much. No matter who he
is. Perhaps there will be some light left for me in this life, not
just the watery dim light of duty and memory. Perhaps I will
forget.   480

HECUBA.
You must never forget. You were blessed above all women.
You must never cease mourning. He was without peer. No one
can ever replace him.

ANDROMACHE.
He's gone! He's gone! He left me here in this agony and
shame. I envy him! He feels no pain, he cannot be disgraced   485
He is free. How am I to live?

HECUBA. You will live in gratitude and service to his memory.

ANDROMACHE. Without joy?

HECUBA. Without joy.

ANDROMACHE. Without hope?   490

HECUBA. Without hope.

ANDROMACHE.
The dead ask too much of us. I cannot do it. I will find a
way to love life. Even in slavery. Even in bondage and

degradation. It is only my body that can be owned.
My mind, my spirit belongs to me. 495

HECUBA. You who were so blessed in that marriage.

ANDROMACHE.
I was blessed before I ever saw him. I was blessed to be
given life. It is a gift. I cannot throw it back with disgust
because he was taken away from me. I must learn to love it.
Even in this horror. Even in this nightmare. Even without him. 500
Far from home. I will find a way.
Oh, Hector, I loved you!

HECUBA.
You were a good wife and a sweetness in his life. And you
have given me my only grandchild. Be careful and raise him
well in his new home. Teach him to remember. Tell him 505
about his father. Murmur stories of us quietly into his ear
when he sleeps so he will dream of his father's city, shining
again, high on its parapets. And let him come back to the
hollow shell of this place and raise it again, long after all
of us are dead. Let him raise his father's city from the ashes 510
and neglect of history. Let him marry well and have many
children and let these walls echo with Trojan laughter once
again. *(Looks at the child.)* Will you do that? For me?
For your father? Then we will live again.

WOMEN.
Then we will live on. 515

(They cluster around the child.)

Yes, we will live on.
You will do this, little one.
In your memory, we will live.

(The WOMEN turn. TALTHYBIUS, a Greek soldier, enters.)

TALTHYBIUS. Do not hate me.

HECUBA. You are only a Greek. Give me more reason. 520

TALTHYBIUS.
I speak for others. They sent me here to… I can't say.

ANDROMACHE.
What could you possibly do to us that is worse than what has
already been done? Kill us? We would sleep in surrender of
our misery. Rape us? We are already tagged for parcel to our
different rapes. There is nothing we have left to fear. 525

TALTHYBIUS. I have come for the child.

HECUBA. Which child?

TALTHYBIUS. Dead Hector's child.

ANDROMACHE.
Must he go to another master than the one I serve?

TALTHYBIUS.
There is no way to say this—the council decreed...   530

ANDROMACHE.
What? Must he be left behind in the ruined city, all alone?

TALTHYBIUS. Worse, terrible. I can't say it.

ANDROMACHE. What did the council decree?

TALTHYBIUS. That he must die.

HECUBA. How?   535

TALTHYBIUS.
He must be hurled from the battlements of Troy. The top
of the city walls.

    (ANDROMACHE *clings to the child and moves as if to resist.*)

(*To* HECUBA:) You must reason with her. It will only be worse
if she resists.

HECUBA. You talk to her.   540

TALTHYBIUS.
Lady. Please. Let it happen. No one can help you. No one can
save him now. There is no shame in submission at this time.
You've lost. Your city, your army, your protectors gone. It
will be better for you, it will be better for him to just give
him over. He will not know. Do not let him hear his mother's   545
cry. He will not understand. And it will be quick. A moment
in the blinding air and then it will be over. Lady. Give over.

HECUBA.
Let her speak to him. Let her have him alone, for the last time.

TALTHYBIUS. She has that right.

    (ANDROMACHE *cradles the child.*)

ANDROMACHE.
You smell so sweet. My dear baby. My dear baby.   550
You smell so sweet. I knew you were coming to me so long
before my belly swelled. I thought: My son! My son! He will
rule the world. And you arrived shining like a conqueror.

And through all my pain I looked at your face and laughed.
Great Hector's shining son! 555
Oh, let me smell your downy head once more. My darling boy.
Your arms, your belly, your feet, your eyes, your lips.
There is all the joy of life in you. All the hope.
You are all and only happiness.

(TALTHYBIUS *takes the child and exits.*)

Greeks! Savages! Murderers! 560
What has he done to you? That tiny child?
What are you afraid of? He's a baby!
I have no strength to save my only child.
It has come to this.
Oh, Zeus! Can you look down on this? 565
Can you look down on this?
Where are the gods who loved us?
My arms are empty.
I can walk now,
I am light now 570
Nothing to carry
I can walk down to the ships
And find the passage away from this cursed place.

(ANDROMACHE *exits.*)

WOMEN.
They still tell the stories. About the blessed city. 575
That when the gods walked the earth
They walked here in Troy.

HECUBA. I told you that story. I was raised on that story.

WOMEN.
No city on earth as splendid as ours.
No city so beloved by the gods. 580
The palaces were built of gold.
The streets were wide and lovely.
When the harvest was good they said
Some god has breathed on our fields.
I was told that one of my ancestors was a god. 585
And I.
And I.
Even when they stormed the city
Even when the battlements were on fire
It was never hot inside the walls 590
There was always a cool breeze
And the scent of flowers

We are blessed. Troy is blessed.
That's what I always thought.
That's what I was told. 595

HECUBA.
That's what I was told.
Oh, Gods!
I don't want to live through the moments that are coming.
I don't want to feel the suffering that is on its way.
Why do I still call on you? 600
I say your names still and feel protected
Just a childish habit
But still I call for you.

WOMEN.
We have lost the way of pleasing God.
You cannot care for us anymore. 605
You watch us and do nothing.
We built you temples.
We have burnt incense at your altars.
Sacrificed every day.
All the flowers I grew 610
And offered up to you.
The tree I planted
That gave apples every year.
All of what I viewed as sacred
You have betrayed. 615

(TALTHYBIUS *enters carrying the child on Hector's shield.*)

TALTHYBIUS.
I washed the blood off in the river that still flows through the
city. And I found the shield. His father's shield. It was a great
war prize. But I took it and laid him on it. I will go dig the
grave and then we must go.

(TALTHYBIUS *exits.*)

HECUBA.
Such a little child still. So small. 620
And to think that I had planned your wedding already.
Saw it all so clearly. The flowers and shouts.
Because you would have been a king.
And when you died, late in life,
your family and people around you, 625
You would lie in state
Mourned by half the world.
Find something to cover him.

WOMEN.
Here.
I found something.   630
There's enough to wrap him in.
This will do.

    (The WOMEN wrap the body in scraps of their own clothing.)

HECUBA.
Not that it matters to him.
His head is broken as an egg.
Oh, dark butcher Death.   635
You closed your eyes and swung wild.
I have seen the end of all my children.
Oh, my dear women, Troy was not meant to last.
All that we have loved has vanished from the quickening air.

WOMEN.
The dead are safe in their nothingness.   640
It is we, captive in our own broken hearts,
Who must breathe and run, breathe and run.
Troy!
We will track your ashes throughout the world
And when they ask us where we came from,   645
We will say "nowhere."
Nowhere.

HECUBA.
Children of this city.
Now we are motherless.

WOMEN.
Look! Look! What's that?   650
What are they doing?
Up there, up on the highest towers,
There are men with torches.
See the flame dance along the columns and arches!
All the houses are falling   655
Wall after wall flashes hot and crumbles
There is the city
Breathing her last
Screaming her death cry
Sighing as she falls   660
She is falling
She is falling
Troy is falling

    (TALTHYBIUS enters.)

TALTHYBIUS. To the ships. It is over.

HECUBA. *(Kneeling:)*
You Trojan soil. You that I was laid upon as   665
a newborn baby. You that nursed my mother and her mother's
mother. You that nursed all my children. Hear me!
I call now to the dead. I beat the ground with my hands.
Listen! Listen!

> *(The* WOMEN *kneel and beat the ground.)*

WOMEN.
Listen! Listen!   670
I call to my dead
I call to my love
I call to my husband
My children
My friends!   675

HECUBA. Troy! Troy! Troy!

WOMEN. Troy! Troy! Troy!

HECUBA. We will remember you!

WOMEN. We will remember you!

HECUBA. We will remember you!

WOMEN. We will remember you!   680

> *(A great crack, like thunder, is heard.)*

WOMEN.
What was that?
What was that?
Did you hear?
I heard the city fall.   685
She is gone.
She is gone.
She is gone.

HECUBA.
I dreamed there was a city. Spires glinting in the sun.
Stones cool to the touch, even on the hottest day. A city of   690
such people, such faces, such hands, vivid with language,
with stories, with plans. I dreamed there was a city. My home.
And the sky arched blue above it as if to hold it in its gaze.
As if it would last forever. Great in its history. Famous in
its exploits. Known throughout the world for its fine waters,   695
high vistas and the smell of the sea.

TALTHYBIUS. It's over. We must go.

WOMEN.
We must go.
We must go.

HECUBA. Yes. We must go.   700

    (All exit.)

End of Play